Music Resources Online

Also by Andy McWain

Jazz Practice Ideas with Your Real Book

Make Money Online with Your Music

Music Resources Online

Web Resources for Musicians:
*Music Sales, Distribution, Teaching, Marketing,
Production, Publishing, E-Commerce, and More*

Andy McWain

FULLER STREET
MUSIC & MEDIA

FULLER STREET MUSIC & MEDIA

Music Resources Online
Web Resources for Musicians: Music Sales, Distribution, Teaching, Marketing, Production, Publishing, E-Commerce, and More

The author greatly appreciates you taking the time to read his work. Please leave a review wherever you bought the book.

Thank you for supporting my work.

First Edition: v.1.7
Published by Fuller Street Music & Media.
www.fullerstreetmusic.com

For more information, please visit:
www.musicresourcesonline.com

ISBN-13: 978-0692678992
ISBN-10: 0692678999
First Edition: April 2016

10 9 8 7 6 5 4 3 2 1

For my wonderful wife and our little girl:
You two are amazing. Thank you for everything.

TABLE OF CONTENTS

Introduction

Welcome to MUSIC RESOURCES ONLINE, a collection of the best websites online for musicians. If you're trying to leverage Web 3.0 to promote and sell your music, connect with fans, teach online, write books, sell merchandise, and just make a living as a musician, then this is for you. Collected here is THE list of the most amazing sites, tools, and -- in some cases -- largely untapped resources that can change your career as a musician forever.

I put this together because musicians need an easy way to leverage the web effectively.

This book is the resource guide every 21st-century musician, singer, songwriter, composer, recording engineer, and lyricist needs. It contains links, descriptions, ideas, case studies, and strategies to hundreds of amazing and useful websites all across the web that will help you do more with your music.

These are the TOP music-related sites that everyone should know about -- and this list has been compiled through countless hours of research and from the first-hand use of many of these resources.

- Do you know where to sell your digital recordings online, including cover songs?
- Do you know where to start a blog to promote your music?
- Do you know how to monetize your blog or musician website?
- Do you know where to register your music for worldwide broadcast royalties?
- Do you know where to crowd-fund your next music project or recording?
- Do you know where to teach online where millions of students can find your course materials?
- Do you know where to publish a music ebook, paperback, or audiobook online?

How to Use This Book

This book is designed to be very useful from the first time you use it. You can browse through the listings in alphabetical order, or feel free to skip around, but the real power comes from visiting the sites listed here. For cross-referencing purposes, I also listed some music topics with specific suggestions on which entries to read. (You can also use your e-reader's search function to find others.) I tried to give you an extensive list of resources, but it can never be complete in this format. I have added many sites that I use often, but inclusion in this book should not be considered an endorsement. Please make sure to do your research and due diligence before signing up with any of the websites listed in this book.

For those who don't know the names of many of these music-related websites and resources, alphabetical listings don't help. So feel free to start with the 'Category List' chapter if you have a specific interest. That's where some similar, related sites are listed together so that you can find targeted sources to begin your online explorations.

And for those musicians looking for an actual ACTION PLAN, I decided to include a few hypothetical "Case Studies" at the end of the A-Z Resource List. I wanted to give you an idea how individual readers and musicians might approach these various sites and tools and put some of this new information and knowledge into immediate use.

Lastly, I created this graphic below to inspire you to think broadly about what you can do or sell as a musician to make a living. It's a global marketplace and your music, your products, and your services can now have access to customers all around the planet. Don't just sell a single CD and have a weekend gig... try selling beats, courses, books/ebooks, or running an authority website on your favorite music interests that generates affiliate commissions and passive income. The sky's the limit because there really is a global online economy.

Leverage the possibilities and opportunities of web 3.0 -- use this directory to find new tools, new sites, and new services to unlock music resources that perhaps you never knew existed. Good luck!

Most musicians sell only three things: their performances (gigs/sessions), their recordings (CD/digital), and their time (teaching). The web makes it possible to sell other things more easily -- like music books/ebooks, videos, various courses/teaching, and other products (including referral or affiliate sales).

Here are stats from February 2016 ebook sales on Amazon. These numbers are for the US sales only, but the month included sales in at least ten other countries. Some of the same books sell on Google, Apple, Barnes & Noble, Kobo, and other platforms, as well.

Net Units Sold
0
1
10
1
1
1
2
10
1
115
7
1
1
1
10
7
1
4
1

Chapter One: A to C

• Ableton
What is it?: A music software company.
For musicians: Ableton Live is one of the premiere digital audio workstations (DAW) and probably one of the tools that every musician, composer, arranger, and music educator needs to learn.
Website: www.ableton.com

• ACX
What is it?: The resource for audiobook publishing, and another Amazon company.
For musicians: Use this site to publish an audiobook version of your independently published ebook or paperback on Audible, Amazon, and iTunes. Also, for singers, voice-over artists, and recording studios, the site features a marketplace to become an audiobook producer or audition for titles seeking audiobook production.
Website: www.acx.com

• Amazon
What is it?: One of the world's largest e-commerce platforms.
For musicians: One of the most versatile places to make money online for musicians (see below). It's also a platform to sell your

music (CDs and more) as well as digital downloads (mp3s).
Website: www.amazon.com

• Amazon Associates Program
What is it?: Amazon pays web publishers (you!) an affiliate
commission (4-8%, higher on individual items) for sending referral
traffic to Amazon.
For musicians: You can make money by referring your fans
from your website(s) to Amazon.com to buy your latest CD,
book, or other merchandise. The bonus is that you will receive a
commission on any purchases the customer makes during the same
visit.
Website: affiliate-program.amazon.com

• Amazon FBA / Marketplace
What is it?: These are the programs that allow everyone to sell on
Amazon.
For musicians: Whether you sell merchant-fulfilled (you ship it!)
or FBA (Fulfillment by Amazon), it's possible to sell on Amazon
-- either music products you create, buy wholesale, or arbitrage, or
private label items that you have manufactured and branded with
your logo. Many avenues for selling on their massive platform in
multiple countries.
Website: sellercentral.amazon.com

• Amazon KDP
What is it?: Amazon's Kindle Direct Publishing, the site to help
indie authors publish their ebooks onto Amazon's global platform.
For musicians: Ebooks like the one you're reading can be published
on KDP and pay author's and indie publishers a royalty rate of
either 35% or 70%. You create the content, and the with Amazon's
online distribution your ebooks are available on their platforms
in thirteen countries: United States, Canada, United Kingdom,
Germany, Netherlands, Spain, Italy, France, Mexico, Brazil,
Japan, India, and Australia.
Website: kdp.amazon.com

• Apple iBooks
What is it?: Another major tech company offering distribution of your ebooks.
For musicians: Apple is another global brand that allows indie writers and publishers (musicians!) to publish their ebooks online. With their global reach, Apple's platform makes your new product available in 51 countries.
Website: itunesconnect.apple.com

• AppSumo
What is it?: A website to find digital deals for promotion, marketing, and more.
For musicians: They have incredible deals on tools, resources, software, utilities, and more to help you run your musician website, promote your band or learn about internet marketing and more
Website: www.appsumo.com

• ArtistShare
What is it?: Record label that crowd-sources new projects with unique bonus content
For musicians: not only is it an inspiring Grammy-winning record label with major recording artists, but there's also a lot of bonus content on the site from the artists as a way of crowdfunding their new projects. For professional development, it's a great place to find lessons, tutorials, sketches, and behind the scenes videos by professional musicians and recording artists
Website: www.artistshare.com

• Asana
What is it?: Asana is a web/mobile application for teamwork and collaborations, without using email.
For musicians: This is a dynamic site to use for collaborative projects of any type. It's also free for "teams" up to 15 members. Use your imagination.
Website: www.asana.com

• ASCAP
What is it?: The American Society of Composers, Authors, and Publishers is a performing rights society.
For musicians: Join a performing rights society to earn royalties on your compositions that are being broadcast (radio, television, and more) or performed in certain paid concerts.
Website: www.ascap.com

• Audiam
What is it?: Audiam is the company that helps artists get paid when their music is used with videos on YouTube.
For musicians: Key player in helping you make money on YouTube, Spotify, Google Play, Rhapsody, Beats, and Amazon Prime
Website: www.audiam.com

❋

• BandCamp
What is it?: BandCamp is a place for artists, fans, or labels to sign up and share music
For musicians: BandCamp is a great place online to sell your music because of real time stats, simple preorders, a combination of physical and digital products, and the ability to sell in about 18 currencies. It's free for artists, and $20 per month for labels to sign up.
Website: www.bandcamp.com

• BandPage
What is it?: A place online for musicians and bands to maintain their profile, videos, tracks, and tour dates.
For musicians: Because of the massive number of fans who access the site and the updates that BandPage makes across the web (Facebook, Twitter, SoundCloud, VEVO, and more), this site helps you find more fans and sell more music
Website: www.bandpage.com

• Blogger
What is it?: A free blogging platform owned by Google.
For musicians: If you need a simple blog, Blogger is a solid choice
that allows for a small amount of customization, including custom
domains purchased through the dashboard. It's also possible to
monetize your blogger music blog with Google's Adsense ads.
Website: www.blogger.com

• Blogging Platforms
See entries for: Blogger (above), Medium, Weebly, and Wix

• Bluehost
What is it?: A reliable web hosting company.
For musicians: If you want to build a website, or multiple music-
related sites on a single shared hosting account, then you need
a provider like Bluehost. [Yes this is what I use for my sites.
This hosting referral link includes a free domain: http://bit.ly/
hostingacct
Website: www.bluehost.com

• BMI
What is it?: An American performing rights society
For musicians: Like ASCAP and SESAC, BMI is where
composers, lyricists, songwriters, and publishers register their
works to collect royalties for radio, television, and other broadcasts,
as well as some streaming and live performances.
Website: www.bmi.com

• Bookbaby
What is it?: A company that helps sell your print books and ebooks
online
For musicians: This is another outlet for musicians to create indie
publishing projects to collect royalties, sell direct on their website,
and add another revenue stream.
Website: www.bookbaby.com

• BookBub
What is it?: BookBub is the premiere ebook promotion site.
For musicians: For indie publishing, BookBub is a paid promotion powerhouse. They maintain mailing lists with millions of active ebook readers divided into genre categories.
Website: www.bookbub.com

• Booklaunch
What is it?: Booklaunch helps authors create a separate landing page for every book, with basic plans starting at no cost.
For musicians: If you've written a music book, here's a place to promote it. A professional template site like this helps generate additional sales, as well as helps your book in search engine ranking.
Website: www.booklaunch.io

✳

• CafePress
What is it?: Create unique gifts, posters, mugs, and t-shirts.
For musicians: With a simple upload, it's easy to create band, label, artist, or music project products. When your fans buy these items, they can help you promote your projects, and you'll earn a commission.
Website: www.cafepress.com

• CDbaby
What is it?: CDbaby is an independent music retailer to help you sell compact discs and digital downloads.
For musicians: Selling music at CDbaby gives you a dashboard for physical and digital sales across all of the major platforms (Amazon, iTunes, Spotify, etc.), as well as on the site itself.
Website: www.cdbaby.com

• Chitika
What is it?: This is an online ad serving company.

For musicians: If you run a music site or blog, and you want to monetize the site with paid ads (CPC "Cost Per Click", and CPM "Cost Per Thousand" Views), Chitika is one of the alternatives to Google AdSense.
Website: www.chitika.com

• CJ Affiliate by Conversant
What is it?: CJ Affiliate is where you sign up for referral relationships with a broad range of companies.
For musicians: To monetize a website, blog site, or other music site, CJ Affiliate by Conversant is a dashboard utility to access referral relationships. You submit your site URL, describe its purpose (blog, e-commerce, etc.), and then apply for the ability to promote products from music retailers, sheet music stores, and more.
Website: www.cj.com

• ClickBank
What is it?: ClickBank is a digital products sales platform.
For musicians: If you've created a course, reference materials, or any digital product, you can sell it through ClickBank, and make it available anywhere on the web. Additionally, you can sign up to be an affiliate for other people's digital products (including music-related products), and earn referral commissions, sometimes as high as 50%.
Website: www.clickbank.com

• Craigslist
What is it?: A marketplace for goods and services with regional boards throughout the country and around the globe.
For musicians: Besides being an outlet to buy and sell used music gear, Craigslist always maintains a musicians community area where bands and musicians can network. There are also arbitrage opportunities by purchasing used music gear locally and selling for a profit nationally/internationally on sites like eBay, Amazon, and elsewhere.
Website: www.craigslist.org

• CreateSpace

What is it?: CreateSpace is an Amazon-owned print on demand company.

For musicians: You can make a paperback book, CD, or DVD, and CreateSpace will only print or manufacture it when someone has ordered it.

Your products then sell in the United States, Canada, United Kingdom, Germany, France, Spain, and Italy.

Website: www.createspace.com

Chapter Two: D to F

• Discmakers
What is it?: Established CD manufacturer with on-site mastering, graphic design, and duplication.
For musicians: Great place to get your CDs and DVDs made, and for an extra fee their experienced art department can create professional-looking products for all genres of music. They have partnerships with other companies to simplify digital and physical sales options.
Website: www.discmakers.com

• Distrokid
What is it?: Distrokid is a digital music aggregator.
For musicians: A simple platform to get your wav, mp4, and other audio tracks uploaded to iTunes, Google Play, Spotify, Tidal, and others. The site charges flat fees for one artist, two artists, or labels and doesn't take royalties on digital music sales. Their pricing model encourages musicians to be prolific.
Website: www.distrokid.com

• Ditto Music
What is it?: DittoMusic is a digital music aggregator.

For musicians: Flat pricing for singles and albums, with no percentage royalties taken, to distribute your music onto 200 stores.
Website: www.dittomusic.com

• Draft2Digital
What is it?: Ebook aggregator
For musicians: If you've written an ebook, you may likely be selling it only at Amazon.com. Draft2Digital is an easy, one-stop aggregator that can get your ebook ePub file on Barnes & Noble, Apple iBooks, Scribd, Tolino, Oyster, and Inktera.
Website: www.draft2digital.com

✳

• eBay
What is it?: Major e-commerce marketplace for new and used products.
For musicians: Not only is eBay a great place to find used gear, sheet music, recordings, etc., it's also a good place to earn extra money. Some musicians simply sell their own personal music stuff, but it's also possible to buy music gear at yard sales, thrift stores, on Craigslist, etc., and resell it on eBay.
Website: www.ebay.com

• Ebookit
What is it?: Ebookit is an indie ebook aggregator and service company.
For musicians: Not only with Ebookit help you get your writing projects on multiple sales platforms, but they also provide editing, graphic design, and paperback book layout services.
Website: www.ebookit.com

• Etsy
What is it?: E-commerce platform for handmade, vintage, and crafts-related products.

For musicians: For unique band or artist merchandise, Etsy is a sales channel for hand-crafted products.
Website: www.etsy.com

• EverNote
What is it?: Website and app for tagged organizational note taking.
For musicians: For content, music, ideas, inspiration, photos, documents, and general backup, EverNote is an organizational tool that synchronizes across devices.
Website: www.evernote.com

✳

• Fandalism
What is it?: A site to network with other musicians.
For musicians: If you're searching for musicians who play or sing a specific style of music within 10 to 1000 miles of a specific location, Fandalism is the networking site designed for that. If you're looking for collaborators, you can post a performance video and other musicians can follow, comment, or contact you.
Website: www.fandalism.com

• Fiverr
What is it?: Micro-job service platform.
For musicians: For buyers, Fiverr is a place to hire everything from graphic design, editing, website, promotional gigs. There are also some musicians who will provide one-off recording services. For sellers, Fiverr is a good place to post your gigs related to music engraving, transcribing, arranging, tracking, and more.
Website: www.fiverr.com

Chapter Three: G to I

• Google Adsense
What is it?: Adsense is a paid ad-serving function of Google.
For musicians: If you have a musician blog site, content site, or authority site that you're trying to monetize, a Google Adsense account will serve up text, graphic, and video-based ads to your readers. These ads are related to the content of your site and also the readers browsing history.
Website: www.google.com/adsense/start/

• Google Hangouts
What is it?: This is google's video chat service, integrated with both Google Plus and YouTube.
For musicians: This is a great way for more than one person to have a public video chat, encourage fans to participate, and record discussions for archiving on YouTube (Hangouts on Air).
Website: www.google.com/hangouts

• Google Drive
What is it?: This is Google's extremely useful online apps and cloud sharing site.
For musicians: Google Drive is an online resource to create and

share documents, slides/presentations, and spreadsheets.
Website: drive.google.com

• Google Play Store
What is it?: Google's platform to sell music, apps, and ebooks.
For musicians: Selling products on any global platform as large
as Google is a good way to make broad sales in a number of
countries. Whether it's music, ebooks, or apps, musicians can find
customers at busy sites like this. The Google Books Partner Center
lets you publish ebooks direct to their platforms with simple ePub
files.
Website: play.google.com

• GoOnWrite
What is it?: Go On Write is a pre-made ebook cover service.
For musicians: If you've written an ebook (or paperback), here's a
site with relatively inexpensive pre-made ebook covers in a variety
of genres. Browse the available covers, purchase credits, and then
submit your title and author text. Custom ebook design orders, as
well as paperback covers and marketing materials, are available
from these images.
Website: www.goonwrite.com

• Gumroad
What is it?: Here's a site to sell digital downloads of any type.
For musicians: If you need a way to sell a digital course (PDF and
mp3s), charts (pdf files), or any other digital download -- directly
from your site -- check out Gumroad. They take a flat commission
(5% + $0.25) and handle all the credit card or PayPal transactions
while allowing you to create a simple, well-designed sales site on
Gumroad, and pop-up window that embeds into any site.
Website: www.gumroad.com

✳

• HubPages

What is it?: Hubpages is a free article site where freelancers can participate in revenue-sharing.

For musicians: Here's another site to write about any topic that interests you (including reviews), and place ads from Google, and products from Amazon and eBay with your content and share revenue with the site.

Website: www.hubpages.com

✳

• Infobarrel

What is it?: A revenue-sharing passive income article site.

For musicians: Infobarrel also accepts articles and content from freelancer writers and that content are monetized with ads and affiliate products so that the writer and site share in the revenue.

Website: www.infobarrel.com

• IFTTT

What is it?: It's a web service to use, browse, or create simple scripts or 'recipes' between apps.

For musicians: IFTTT, which stands for If This Then That, can simplify social media postings across a couple platforms, search for gear on Craigslist, or store your content automatically. The site contains some user-generated 'recipes' where you can 'automate your online life.' Imagine getting a text about the weather every day, or automatically storing every Instagram photo you post to your Evernote account -- that's the kind of automated task that IFTTT can do. Here's another example: You can automatically post to Facebook every time you put new music on Soundcloud.

Website: www.ifttt.com

• InfoLinks

What is it?: It's an advertising platform that helps website make money.

For musicians: Here's another revenue service if you run a website

or blog and want to get paid for user clicks and impressions.
Website: www.infolinks.com

• Instagram
What is it?: A social media mobile site based on sharing photos, acquired by Facebook in 2012.
For musicians: Another popular social media site with over 300 million active users, Instagram is another place for musicians and bands to create and develop a following online.
Website: www.instagram.com

Chapter Four: J to L

• Kickstarter
What is it?: The crowd-funding site for creative projects.
For musicians: Artists, filmmakers, designers, musicians, and other creative artists propose a project, a funding goal, and a deadline. The Kickstarter project funding is 'all-or-nothing,' meaning unless these proposals are fully funded -- historically 44% on the site -- then they don't go forward.
Website: www.kickstarter.com

• Kobo
What is it?: Toronto-based ebook platform (owned by the Japanese e-commerce company Rakuten).
For musicians: Here's another platform for musicians who have written ebooks. The Kobo global distribution platform makes the titles available in 190 countries.
Website: www.kobo.com/writinglife

✳

• Loudr

What is it?: Digital licensing site and music distribution aggregator.
For musicians: This site makes it simple to not only distribute your
music to online stores and services like Rdio, Deezer, Pandora,
Google Play, Spotify, iTunes, and Amazon mp3, but also integrates
cover song mechanical licensing in the process.
Website: www.loudr.fm

Chapter Five: M to O

• Medium
What is it?: A free blogging platform and social sharing site developed by the founders of Twitter.
For musicians: If you're looking for a place to write online without getting a website or starting a blog, Medium is an easy, elegant site where writers share a range of personal articles. Each post is tagged with an approximate reading time ("5 min read"), and the site gives useful stats about your article's traffic over time. It's a good place to build up a new following, share written content and images with your fan base or reader base, and your posts or articles can be followed by a bio with links out to your other sites, recorded music, and more.
Website: www.medium.com

• Meerkat
What is it?: Twitter-based live streaming app.
For musicians: Once you build up a personal or band following on Twitter, live streaming apps are a way to involve your fans, followers, and others in your live events, rehearsals, behind-the-scenes in the studio, Q&A sessions, and more. It's also a good way to gain new Twitter followers, and invite viewers to visit your other

sites online or to find your recordings for sale. The live stream allows questions, comments, likes, and retweets from anyone watching.
Website: www.meerkatapp.co

• MondoTunes
What is it?: Digital music distribution aggregator.
For musicians: Like some of the other digital music distribution services, MondoTunes gets your music on iTunes and hundreds of other online, mobile, and streaming music partner sites. They also have additional music mastering and marketing premium services.
Website: www.mondotunes.com

• Myspace
What is it?: Social networking site with a focus on music.
For musicians: The original Myspace started in 2003 and lost relevance for a while, but after it was sold to new owners Specific Media Group and Justin Timberlake in 2011, the site is making a comeback. Artists can't specifically make money on Myspace, but it's still a solid promotion and music discovery tool on both desktop and mobile.
Website: www.myspace.com

✳

• OysterBooks
What is it?: A platform to sell ebooks online.
For musicians: Here's another ebook sales platform, that features an unlimited subscription model that allows readers to borrow millions of books. For musicians who have written ebooks, the only way at this point to list your books on Oyster is through an aggregator like Draft2Digital or Smashwords.
Website: www.oysterbooks.com

Chapter Six: P to R

• Patreon
What is it?: This is a crowd-funding platform.
For musicians: Unlike Kickstarter and other single goal
campaigns, Patreon is a recurring support model of crowd-funding
where the creatives get paid on an ongoing basis after posting
more art, music, or content. You could use this to release a new
song, video, or podcast every month, or other creative project.
Website: www.patreon.com

• Performing Rights Societies
See entries: ASCAP, BMI, SESAC

• Periscope
What is it?: Live video streaming and social networking app for
iOS and Android that integrates with Twitter. Bought by Twitter
in March 2015.
For musicians: Like Meerkat, Periscope is a way to stream live
video to your Twitter followers, archive it for later viewing, and to
find new followers.
Website: www.periscope.tv

• Pinterest
What is it?: A social media sharing and discovery site set up like a large visual bulletin board with pictures.
For musicians: Pinterest is one of the social media sites that converts very well from browsers to buyers, so nearly any music-related business needs to have some presence on Pinterest.
Website: www.pinterest.com

• Pixel of Ink
What is it?: Free ebook email promotion service.
For musicians: If you write ebooks, this is one of the bigger direct email marketing platforms for promotions.
Website: www.pixelofink.com

• PledgeMusic
What is it?: PledgeMusic is a direct-to-fan music platform.
For musicians: Sign up for an account to fund a project or pre-order, and offer extras to your fans like photos, autographed sheet music, private performance videos, lessons, house concerts, and more. The site features new indie artists launching new projects alongside some established recording artists funding their latest albums. On a recent visit, there were projects or pre-orders from Soul Asylum, UB40, Claudia Acuna, Macy Gray, Michael Hutchence (from INXS), Megadeth, Allan Holdsworth, Dweezil Zappa, and Veruca Salt, among others.
Website: www.pledgemusic.com

• ProductHunt
What is it?: An amazing site that features new tools, new products, and new technology.
For musicians: Look here for new apps, tools, sites and more for your music and all of your media company needs online.
Website: www.producthunt.com

✳

• Reddit

What is it?: An entertainment, social networking, and news site. For musicians: The massive amount of traffic, information, and links shared on Reddit makes it a perfect place to shares links and posts, although everything on the site gets voted up or down by other users.

Website: www.reddit.com

• ReverbNation

What is it?: Launched in 2006, ReverbNation is a site developed to help musicians develop and manage their careers.

For musicians: Three levels of membership including free, basic, and premium, ReverbNation gives musicians access to festival, labels, and press contacts, and the ability to host an electronic press kit. The higher tiers include up to 100MB song uploads. The Premium tier includes a website, email management, digital distribution, and a custom Android fan app for artists or bands who want all their tools.

Website: www.reverbnation.com

Chapter Seven: S to U

• Seekyt
What is it?: Seekyt is a platform where writers post original articles, posts, and reviews and share in the site's advertising revenue.
For musicians: If you want to write about music, gear, or other interests, joining sites like Seekyt give you a way to generate passive income, while also sending traffic back to your own site or to your music.
Website: www.seekyt.com

• SESAC
What is it?: SESAC, based in Nashville, is the smallest of the big three American performing rights societies.
For musicians: Along with ASCAP and BMI, SESAC collects royalties for composers and publishers whose music has had broadcasts (radio, television, and cable) and certain live performances.
Website: www.sesac.com

• Sibelius
What is it?: Software to compose, arrange, engrave, and share

notated music.

For musicians: This is the best-selling music notation software, and it's used by professional musicians, students, and educators around the globe.

Website: www.avid.com/sibelius

• Skillshare

What is it?: A site to teach and learn online for one flat subscription fee.

For musicians: If you develop a course at Skillshare -- music content or otherwise -- you'll share in the subscription revenues collected on the site -- the "royalty pool." They also pay referral commissions if the teachers bring new students to the site with a specific "teacher referral link."

Website: www.skillshare.com

• Skype

What is it?: Video chat software company owned by Microsoft.

For musicians: For musicians, Skype is an easy way to connect, teach, or consult online, especially with people from all around the globe. It's also possible for each person meeting online to share screens.

Website: www.skype.com

• SnapChat

What is it?: This is a social network with the model of taking a picture or video and adding a caption, then sending it to a friend.

For musicians: For musicians, here's a platform that has more than 2+ billion video views every day. The site also shares that "more than 60% of 13 to 34-year-old smartphone users are Snapchatters." If that cross-section of Americans might be interested in your recordings, then this social media platform might be the right promotion tool for your music.

Website: www.snapchat.com

• SoundCloud

What is it?: A music-sharing site, and audio distribution platform based in Berlin, Germany.

For musicians: Here's a site to gain followers, network with fans, and share music with other artists, musicians, and listeners across the globe. Basic membership is free (Partner tier), but Pro and Premier tiers add more features like better stats, and can have longer or unlimited uploads. The top tier also has revenue sharing monetization with the platform.

Website: www.soundcloud.com

• Spreecast

What is it?: Live streaming video site for multiple hosts and guests.

For musicians: Here's another way to engage your audience live with a streaming video event, either paid or free. It's possible to have multiple "producers" onscreen, as well as a chat stream from all attendees watching the spree. Your archived videos can be downloaded and shared elsewhere later.

Website: www.spreecast.com

• StumbleUpon

What is it?: StumbleUpon is a social sharing site to help build traffic.

For musicians: Musicians can "stumble" their posts, websites, and best content around the web in hopes of attracting a larger audience. Certain content on StumbleUpon gets shared enough that it goes "viral."

Website: www.stumbleupon.com

• Smashwords

What is it?: Online independent digital publishing site and ebook aggregator.

For musicians: Here's a free site to publish ebooks, as well as distribute them to major retailers like Apple iBooks, Barnes & Noble, Kobo, OverDrive, and others.

Website: www.smashwords.com

❋

• TeachersPayTeachers
What is it?: This is a site where educators (K-12, homeschool, and higher ed) share, distribute, and sell teaching materials.
For musicians: If you want to earn money by sharing and selling your music-related teaching materials this is the site. Most of the platform's bestsellers are in categories like reading, science, math, and history, but there is a nice assortment of musical materials for all levels. They require each new seller account to post a free product before listing any items for sale, which also means that there are a lot of resources here to download.
Website: www.teacherspayteachers.com

• Textbroker
What is it?: Here's a site to hire writers or to work as a freelance writer.
For musicians: If you want to earn money doing freelance writing online, here's one of the outlets to get started. If you have a website (or more than one) and need to hire writers to create that content, you can find freelancers here.
Website: www.textbroker.com

• Tumblr
What is it?: It's a social networking and microblogging platform, now owned by Yahoo!.
For musicians: This is a good place to create short posts (even multimedia) to get your content seen by many readers and viewers. The site hosts over 230 million blogs as of this writing.
Website: www.tumblr.com

• Tunecore
What is it?: A digital music distribution and aggregator service founded in 2005.
For musicians: TuneCore is another music distributor that can get your music onto over 150 platforms. For one-time set-up fees, the platform pays 100% of music revenue to the artist.
Website: www.tunecore.com

✳

• Udemy
What is it?: This is a platform for online teaching and learning.
For musicians: If you have an idea for a course with video modules, audio, PDF handouts, and more, Udemy's platform might be a great place to teach. The site boasts over seven million students in 190 countries with 16K instructors contributing to the site. The music categories listed on the site now include instrument and vocal instruction, music techniques, and fundamentals, as well as music production and software tutorials.
Website: www.udemy.com

• Upwork
What is it?: Upwork is a site, formerly known as oDesk, used to hire freelancers and to get paid work online.
For musicians: If you need help with a tech, design, accounting, or other problem, here is where you can go to find a freelancer to hire to help you. If you want to set up an account, it's also a place for you to find work online. You can even hire an off-site VA, or virtual assistant, to help you with tasks that you would rather outsource. On Upwork you post a job you need finished (technical, IT, writing, translating, editing, etc.), and get qualified freelancers from all over the world to respond with their proposals. As a worker, it's a good place to register your freelancing skills (music, writing, production, tech, IT, etc.) and make a profile that lets clients know that you are available for hire.
Website: www.upwork.com

• U.S. Copyright Office
What is it?: This is the public record office of copyright registrations in the United States.
For musicians: This is where you can learn about the true regulations pertaining to your musical copyrights as well as the site to officially register your works.
Website: www.copyright.gov

Chapter Eight: V to Z

• Vimeo
What is it?: Vine is a video-sharing website.
For musicians: One of the many current social media apps to promote your music or band.
Website: www.vimeo.com

• Vine
What is it?: Vine is a free short-form looping video service, now owned by Twitter.
For musicians: One of the many current social media apps to promote your music or band.
Website: www.vine.co

❈

• Weebly
What is it?: Free website platform.
For musicians: If you need a basic website, either completely free or just with your paid domain name, Weebly is an easy interface.
Website: www.weebly.com

• Wordpress
What is it?: Wordpress is a simple, but dynamic web content management platform.
For musicians: This is the standard in website design with thousands of templates. The free version of Wordpress is a blogging platform, but if you have shared hosting, then installing Wordpress allows you to monetize.
Website: www.wordpress.com

✳

• YouTube
What is it?: Global video platform owned by Google.
For musicians: A great place to listen to music, study music, explore new artists, and watch lessons and tutorials. As a YouTube partner, uploading videos is a great way to promote your music projects, or simply monetize your content with ad revenue. YouTube is also becoming a major player in music streaming and licensing royalties.
Website: www.youtube.com

✳

• Zerys
What is it?: Content hiring platform for freelance writers and a wide range of clients.
For musicians: If you want to earn extra money writing content, Zerys allows freelancers to submit a writing sample, earn a score (1-5), and then accept writing gigs from a job board based on your score qualification. Most writing assignments won't be about music or the arts, but it is possible to list your expertise in those areas and accept direct assignments. For musicians working as web masters, it's also possible to hire writers and bloggers at Zerys to create content for you.
Website: www.zerys.com

• Zimbalam

What is it?: A digital music distribution site.

For musicians: Another music distribution aggregator site to get your music listed on nineteen global outlets including Amazon, Tidal, Apple Music, Spotify, and more.

Website: www.zimbalam.com

Chapter Nine: Case Studies

S till overwhelmed by all of these possibilities? I thought it might be useful to provide a few 'recipes,' hypothetical situations, or case studies of how musicians can begin to use this book. To get started, here are a few simple, direct solutions for musicians, singers, composers, music educators, and others. Feel free to mix and match any of the strategies to fit your situation. Consider these case studies as starting points.

Case Study One:

Your band just recorded an EP. You want to release it, distribute it, and promote it beyond your Facebook page. You want digital distribution (mp3s on all the big platforms), but you also want physical CD's to sell at your live gigs. You also need to organize and coordinate your band's efforts, and you'd like to get paid for any radio/TV broadcasts of the original music on your new disc. Distribute mp3s: see Distrokid, BandCamp, or CDbaby; Make CDs: see DiscMakers, Createspace; Promote: see Facebook, Instagram, Medium; YouTube; Twitter; Pinterest; Organize: see Asana, Google Drive, or Evernote; Collect royalties: see ASCAP, BMI, or SESAC.

✳

Case Study Two:

You're busy making music, but you just came up with a great idea for an iPhone or Android app, but you're not a developer. What you need to find is a site to post your project and get proposals from talented freelancers with the skills you need. You want to get a domain name for the app business, build a good website, and have a logo made for you new APP company. Post project: Upwork, Fiverr; Domain names: Godaddy, Namecheap, or BlueHost; Logo design: Fiverr, Craigslist, or Upwork; Website hosting: Free site at Weebly, Blogger; but you decide to build a more professional site for your new app business at BlueHost. (Here's my BlueHost referral link, since they're less than $5 per month for WordPress shared hosting, and they give you a free domain with sign-up: http://bit.ly/hostingacct)

✳

Case Study Three:

You want to teach online to bring in a bit of extra income around your gigs and your other work, but you don't know where to start. You have the skills and even some great ideas about content and lesson plans, but you need students. You could start with a basic website and offer some free short video lessons on the site -- to show your qualifications -- and then provide live video lessons. You could also build a beginner course around your instrument and use it to earn residual teaching revenues while you do other things. Videos: see YouTube and Vimeo; Live lessons: see Skype, Google Hangouts, or SpreeCast (to record and broadcast later); Build a complete instructional course: see Udemy, LearnItLive, or Skillshare.

✳

Case Study Four:

You think it would be fun to write an ebook about the history of a certain kind of music, and notice that there are no books on the topic. You're not even sure where to start. Ebook covers: see Go On Write, Ebookit; Indie Publishing Services and Promotion: see Ebookit; Pixel of Ink, and BookBub; Publishing your ebook online: see Amazon KDP; Apple iBooks; Google Play; Kobo; NookPress (of Barnes & Noble); Draft2Digital; Publishing your paperback: Createspace, Lulu, or BookBaby.

Chapter Ten: Category Lists

• BLOGSITES AND REVENUE-SHARING WRITING SITES
See HubPages, InfoBarrel, Seekyt, Medium, WordPress, Blogger, Weebly, Wix, YouTube (video blogging)

• CROWD-FUNDING, ARTIST SUPPORT SITES
See Kickstarter, Patreon, PledgeMusic, ArtistShare

• EBOOKS, PAPERBACKS, AUDIOBOOKS, AND INDIE PUBLISHING
See Amazon KDP (Kindle Direct Publishing), CreateSpace, ACX, Draft2Digital, OysterBooks, Kobo, Apple iBooks & iTunes Producer, Google Play Books, Barnes & Noble's NookPress, BookBub, BookBaby, BookLauch, Pixel of Ink, eBookit, GoOnWrite, Smashwords

• E-COMMERCE SITES
See Amazon FBA/Marketplace, eBay, Etsy, Craigslist, CafePress

• GRAPHIC DESIGN, PHOTO, ORGANIZATION, AND UTILITIES
See AppSumo, Fiverr, Go On Write, IFTTT, Asana, Copy, Evernote, Google Drive

• HIRING/WORKING AS A FREELANCER, VIRTUAL ASSISTANTS, AND PAID WRITING
See Fiverr, Zerys, UpWork, Textbroker

•MUSIC DIGITAL/PHYSICAL SALES, MANUFACTURING, AND DISTRIBUTION
See Distrokid, CDBaby, Discmakers, Loudr, MondoTunes, DittoMusic

• MUSIC GEAR & SOFTWARE
See Ableton, Sibelius

• MUSIC RIGHTS & ROYALTIES
See ASCAP, BMI, SESAC, Audiam, U.S. Copyright Office

•MUSIC TEACHING ONLINE
See YouTube, SpreeCast, Udemy, GumRoad

• REFERRALS, AFFILIATE SITES, AND AD REVENUE
See Google Adsense, Amazon Affiliate, InfoLinks, CJ Affiliate by Conversant, ClickBank, InfoBarrel, HubPages

• SOCIAL MEDIA & MUSIC MARKETING (FANS & MUSICIANS)
See Facebook, Twitter, Medium, Fandalism, Meerkat, Myspace, Periscope, Pinterest, Reddit, SnapChat, Vine, Tumblr, Instagram

Your Opinion

Share Your Opinion with Others: If you found this book useful, informative, inspiring, or helpful, please consider leaving NOT ONLY an online review where you bought it, but feel free to tell your friends, fellow musicians, music students, and others about it! Share the link to this book on Facebook, Twitter, Google+, and elsewhere. THANK YOU!

And if you want, please feel free to visit my websites musicresourcesonline.com and fullerstreetmusic.com, for more information about the resources and the indie publishing information presented here. If you have any questions, comments, or thoughts that you'd like to share, you can contact me by email at this address: andy@musicresourcesonline.com and also at (617) 528-9715. If you don't reach me, leave a voicemail, and I'll get back to you. [Yes, I just put a telephone number in this book!] Thanks again!

Acknowledgments

This book was made possible, in part, because of countless discussions with professional musicians I know and work with, as well as discussions with music capstone students and alumni from the University of Massachusetts-Dartmouth, as well as my music faculty colleagues. The questions asked, and the issues raised gave a lot of this online research its direction! I would also like to thank Neal Bogosian, Michael Caglianone, Chris Poudrier, Jim Robitaille, Marcelle Gauvin, Mark Rasmussen, Ryan Levesque, Chris Green, 'Von Money', Derek Doepker, Kareem Roustom, Abby McWain, and Chris Lopes for their input, encouragement, and other discussions which were useful for me as I thought about the full range of ideas presented here.

About the Author

Jazz pianist and composer Andy McWain has taught jazz theory, improvisation, jazz history courses, jazz ensembles, and applied jazz piano at the University of Massachusetts Dartmouth for several years. He also runs their senior music capstone course that helps graduating music students research and plan for their professional music careers as they complete their degree program. McWain studied music at UMass-Dartmouth (B.M.), the Aspen Music School, and earned his M.M. in composition from the New England Conservatory of Music in Boston. His principal teachers included Lee Hyla, Michael Gandolfi, and Zhou Long for composition, and Anders Boström, John Harrison III, and Charlie Banacos for jazz improvisation.

Andy McWain received honors and fellowships for his music from the American Music Center, the American Composers Forum, the Atlantic Center for the Arts, ASCAP, the Massachusetts Cultural Council, the Akiyoshidai International Art Village, and Yaddo. His recordings as a leader and co-leader [Starfish, Vigil, Resemblance, and Interpreter] on the indie Fuller Street Music label, feature mostly free jazz, avant-garde, collective improvisations, and original music. His most recent recordings include Andy McWain Ensemble "Live at Audible Think" and "Mishawum."

"My playing, performing, recording, and teaching has taken me throughout the United States, across Europe, and into Asia. With my writing, I'm happy to share what I've learned along the way with you." More information, other books on music, and other resources can be found at the site: http://www.fullerstreetmusic. com and http://www.musicresourcesonline.com.

Author's Note

Thanks for checking out my newest book for musicians, and also for reading these 'behind the scenes' author's notes. I've wanted to start a reference book like this for a while because musicians usually just need some idea of where to go online to begin selling their music. Feel free to join our Facebook group listed below, and also check out our new site at: musicresourcesonline.com.

A book like this -- claiming to be a comprehensive directory of online music resources -- needs some clarification. It's not an academic book filled with music resources for higher education. It's not filled with granting agencies, foundations, summer festivals, music conservatories, graduate programs, and more. (Okay, now that I've thought about it, that would be useful stuff too, but many of those things are one-time opportunities for musicians.)

In my own personal development as a musician, I attended a few jazz workshops, several composer workshops, a couple fellowship and residency opportunities, and more. And those things changed my entire musical world. But they often meant spending money (at least on travel), and even if they were completely free (Japan!), they did not necessarily contribute to direct change in my musical income or livelihood. I grew as an artist, and I'm grateful for all of those opportunities, but they are not meant to help you create income streams.

This book contains online opportunities for musicians that are very different than those. This book contains entrepreneurial ways for you to make a living online, or a partial living, or maybe even some much-needed supplemental income. (If you're willing to put in the effort, this book shows you where to look!) I put together these online resources for musicians so that your new revenue streams, royalties, sales, online teaching, and more may be just enough extra income to buy you all the musical freedom you need.

Good luck and thanks again! - AJM

Be sure to join (and participate in) our free
MUSIC RESOURCES ONLINE Facebook Group:
www.facebook.com/groups/musicresourcesonline

MUSIC RESOURCES
O N L I N E

About Fuller Street Music & Media

Fuller Street Music & Media (www.fullerstreetmusic.com) is an indie publisher in Massachusetts (USA) that has released a range of digital and physical products (CDs/mp3s, books, ebooks) across several platforms. FSM started as an ASCAP-affiliated music publisher and small music service company for live performances in New England. FSMM later evolved into a co-op indie recording label that released a range of improvised, free jazz, avant-garde, and creative music recordings by a handful of regional artists. (These recordings are available at all the major music retailers online). Later FSMM developed into its current media company model with several web properties online and as the publisher of a growing catalog of [largely music] ebooks, paperbacks, and musician notebooks (www. incrediblyusefulnotebooks.com).